D0064973

high-tech military weapons

TANK OF TOMORROW

STRYKER

Larry Hama and Bill Cain

HIGH
interest
books

Children's Press®
A Division of Scholastic Inc.
New York / Toronto / London / Auckland / Sydney
Mexico City / New Delhi / Hong Kong
Danbury, Connecticut

Book Design: Erica Clendening
Contributing Editor: Karl Bollers
Photo Credits: Cover, title page Spc. Clinton Tarzia/U.S. Army; pgs. 4, 7
Sgt. Jeremiah Johnson/U.S. Army; pg. 8 © Bettmann/Corbis; pg. 10 © Ronald S.
Haeberle/Time Life Pictures/Getty Images; pg. 12 Spc. David J. Nunn/U.S. Army;
pg. 14 © Fred Ramage/Keystone/Getty Images; pgs. 15, 34 © Cris Bouroncle/
AFP/Getty Images; pg. 16 Sgt. Lisa Jendry/U.S. Army; pg. 17 © Ghaith
Abdul-Ahad/Getty Images; pg. 18 © Maurico Lima/AFP/Getty Images; pg. 20 ©
A. Y. Owen/Time Life Pictures/Getty Images; pg. 22 © Kim Jae-Hwan/AFP/Getty
Images; pg. 24 Airman 1st Class Patrick D. Thorn/U.S. Air Force; pgs. 27, 33
Tech Sgt. John M. Foster/U.S. Army; pg. 30 Jason Kaye/U.S. Army; pg. 36 © Cris
Bouroncle/AFP Photo; pg. 37 © Karim Sahib/AFP Photo; pgs. 38-39 U.S. Army

Library of Congress Cataloging-in-Publication Data

Hama, Larry.
  Tank of Tomorrow: Stryker / Larry Hama and Bill Cain.
  p. cm. — (High-tech military weapons)
  Includes index.
  ISBN-10: 0-531-12094-5 (lib. bdg.)   0-531-18710-1 (pbk.)
  ISBN-13: 978-0-531-12094-1 (lib. bdg.)   978-0-531-18710-4 (pbk.)
  1. Stryker armored vehicle—Juvenile literature. 2. Stryker brigade combat
teams—Juvenile literature. I. Title II. Series

  UG446.5.C24 2007
  623.7'475-dc22

                                                    2006014496

CONTENTS

U.S. soldiers patrol the streets of Iraq in and alongside the light armored vehicle Stryker.

F allujah is a dangerous city. Top secret reports show that terrorists use this Iraqi city just west of Baghdad as a headquarters. These terrorists have been attacking American soldiers from their hideout there. Today, you will spearhead a mission to stop those attacks.

You and your soldiers roll into the city inside four armored vehicles. Your mission is to capture the terrorists hiding there. Suddenly, a violent explosion rocks the vehicle you are traveling in. A terrorist has just launched a rocket-propelled grenade at it. The explosion does not hurt you or the soldiers inside, though.

Within seconds, a high-tech digital communications device helps you to find the shooter. You immediately send the information to the other armored vehicles in your group.

Now you are all on the same page. The other vehicles surround the shooter.

More terrorists emerge to make their last stand. They fire their rifles, but the bullets just bounce off your vehicles' armor. You order the terrorists to drop their weapons. The fight is over. They surrender. Their weapons cannot match the might at your fingertips.

Congratulations, soldier! You just completed a successful combat mission. You commanded a platoon using the Stryker, the U.S. Army's new light armored vehicle (LAV).

Soldiers emerge from the Stryker vehicle and surround a building suspected of harboring terrorists.

In the years leading up to World War II, Adolph Hitler and his Nazi Party transformed Germany into a fascist nation.

chapter 1

STRYKER: WHAT IS IT GOOD FOR?

World War II (1939–1945) was a global conflict that forever changed the face of the planet. Among the war's many results was the defeat of fascism in Europe. Fascism is a form of government in which a dictator and the dictator's political party have complete power over a country. After the United States and its allies won the war, the U.S. military began planning the fight against communism. Communism is a way of organizing a country so that the lands, houses, factories, etc. belong to the government, with profits shared by all.

At the time, communism was believed to be the next major threat to the country. Russia (then called the Soviet Union) was a communist nation and the United States' main enemy. The conflict that resulted is known as

Army helicopters drop off a company of U.S. troops near the Vietnamese village of My Lai.

the cold war. The U.S. and Soviet Union never fought each other directly. Instead, they involved themselves in wars that used third parties. The Soviet Union's army was much bigger than the U.S. Army. The U.S. Army needed big tanks and heavy artillery to compete.

GUERILLA WARFARE

In cold war conflicts such as the Korean War (1950–1953) and the Vietnam War (1954–1975), the U.S. military first encountered guerilla warfare. A guerilla is a member of a small group of fighters who often launch surprise attacks against an official army. They are sneaky and do not organize like an army. They might not use tanks or airplanes. They might not even dress in military uniforms. This does not mean they are not very dangerous.

When the Soviet Union broke up in 1991, communism no longer posed a threat to the United States. Instead, there was an increase in guerilla fighting, and suddenly big tanks and heavy artillery didn't seem so useful. The military knew it would have to adapt to defeat this new enemy and needed both the speed and firepower to do so.

SPECIAL UNITS

The U.S. Army already has units that are specially trained to move quickly, like airborne paratroopers (soldiers who jump out of airplanes with parachutes). They take their equipment with them and jump into dangerous places.

Since paratroopers must carry their equipment, the equipment must be light. Paratroopers are forced to trade strength for speed. As a result, they cannot complete all the combat missions necessary to keep peace.

Other army units depend upon more powerful weapons. These include tanks and infantry armored vehicles. An infantry is the part of an army that fights on foot. These heavy units, however, cannot get to a combat area

Although tanks are effective in combat, they cannot be quickly transported to a war zone because of their weight.

very quickly. In addition to this problem, tanks weigh too much to be flown on airplanes.

SWIFT AND DEADLY

The army needed to find a way to combine a swift reaction with powerful weapons. This would be the best way to fight and win modern wars. The army decided to create a unit that could move anywhere in the world within 96 hours, or four days. It would have to be light enough to be transported–soldiers, equipment, and all–on an airplane. The unit would also have to pack the power of a tank. To create such a unit meant creating new types of combat equipment as well.

THE BCT

The brigade combat team (BCT) is the first unit to meet these challenges. A brigade is an army unit. This particular unit combines speed and lightness of weight with fighting power and ability to survive in battle. The army will eventually create six BCTs. They will be able to fight anywhere in the world. The main vehicle for the BCT is known as the Stryker.

TANKS FOR THE MEMORIES

Great Britain was the first country to develop tanks during World War I (1914–1918), but France, Germany, and the United States soon followed suit. To maintain the project's secrecy, machinery workers were told they were building "water-carriers." This was how the tank got its name.

The Spanish Civil War (1936–1939) showed that heavy tanks would be needed to withstand tank-against-tank combat. In 1939, medium-sized tanks weighed 20 tons (18 metric tons). By 1945, they could weigh up to 45 tons (41 metric tons)!

A brigade combat team travels across the desert plains of northern Iraq with several Stryker armored vehicles in the lead.

SPECIAL FEATURES

With eight wheels instead of heavy tank treads, the Stryker offers mobility and protection in populated areas. The Stryker has a maximum speed of 60 miles (97 km) per hour compared to tanks, which average 43 miles (70 km) per hour. As a result, it can quickly move soldiers to important battlefield positions.

The Stryker has many special features. It can be carried directly to a battle site on a plane.

A Stryker Infantry Carrier Vehicle rolls out of the back of a military transport at Korea's Osan Air Base.

Further, it can be driven out the back of the plane in battle-ready condition once it lands. The Stryker uses high-tech digital communications to find the enemy. It has armor protection so the soldiers inside will not be hurt during attacks. The Stryker is large enough to carry nine soldiers. It can dig in to fight or it can crush and knock down walls.

The Stryker is quiet compared to a tank because it runs on wheels instead of metal treads. It also gathers important information about the enemy from other electronic equipment. It can link to the army's most advanced computers. All of these features help its operating unit move as a fast and powerful combat team.

A network of computers help soldiers aboard the Stryker monitor dangerous areas without ever having to leave the vehicle.

A platoon of Stryker vehicles looks for terrorists amid the streets of a northern Iraqi city.

TWO STRYKERS

The U.S. military often names weapons after soldiers. The army named one of its tanks after General Creighton Abrams. General Abrams served in World War II. He later became the army's chief of staff. The army named its best infantry vehicle after General Omar Bradley. General Bradley was a five-star general. The Stryker is named after two soldiers who each won the Congressional Medal of Honor, Private First Class (PFC) Stuart S. Stryker and Specialist Four (SPC) Robert Stryker.

PFC Stuart Stryker served in the 17th Airborne Division during World War II. On December 11, 1945, his unit tried to attack German headquarters where three American soldiers were being held prisoner, but could not advance because of enemy gunfire. Without regard for his own safety, PFC Stryker rushed to the front of his unit to lead a desperate charge. His bravery inspired the other soldiers

MEDAL MEN

The highest award that military personnel can receive is the Congressional Medal of Honor. Congress created the Medal of Honor in 1862. A soldier must do something above and beyond the call of duty to earn the Medal of Honor. It is often awarded to soldiers after they have died. Of the millions of men and women who have served in the military since 1862, less than thirty-five hundred earned the Medal of Honor.

to follow suit, racing through a hail of bullets. PFC Stryker was struck by gunfire and killed, but the rest of his unit was able to successfully capture enemy headquarters and rescue the American prisoners.

RUMBLE IN THE JUNGLE

SPC Robert Stryker served with the 1st Infantry Division in the Vietnam War. On November 7, 1967, guerillas attacked his unit while they were moving through a dense jungle. As they exchanged gunfire, SPC Stryker realized that the enemy was trying to surround his unit and cut them off from the main body of the army.

Reacting quickly, he began firing grenades at the enemy. This allowed his unit to make it past the enemy and rejoin the larger friendly force. Then SPC Stryker noticed that six wounded members of his unit were dangerously close to an enemy mine. Completely disregarding his own safety, he threw himself on the mine as it exploded. SPC Stryker was killed by the blast, but he died protecting his fellow soldiers.

Robert and Stuart Stryker came from different families. They did not know each other, but shared the same last name. The bravery of these two foot soldiers–the very people the Stryker vehicle is designed to protect–inspired the army to name its new light armored vehicle in honor of them.

During a training exercise in South Korea, the Stryker's off-road capabilities are put to the test.

chapter 3

OFF-ROAD WARRIOR

There are many advantages to having the Stryker instead of a big, heavy vehicle. It is faster and can go 300 miles (483 km) on 53 gallons of fuel. That is a very long distance in a combat zone. The Stryker is fast and easy to repair. It helps keep soldiers safe during combat. The Stryker's tires can be inflated or deflated from inside the vehicle. They can be changed quickly and safely when going from deep mud to a hard road, making it able to cover different types of terrain, or ground. The Stryker has run-flat tires so that even if the tires are completely flat, it can keep going.

The Stryker runs more quietly than heavy armored infantry vehicles do. This increases its stealth and makes it harder for the enemy to detect. Even though it is quiet, the Stryker is still very powerful. It can be used to attack and even destroy an enemy.

Trucks can transport the Stryker on roads. Trucks aren't usually driven into a war zone, however. Soldiers generally get to dangerous places by plane. The military uses many different kinds of airplanes to carry soldiers and equipment.

The most common ones are the C-5, the C-17, and the C-130 Hercules. The C-5 can carry

Although the C-5 (pictured here) can carry more Stryker vehicles than the C-130 Hercules, the smaller Hercules can help them reach their destination faster.

up to seven Strykers. The C-17 carries up to four. The Hercules can only carry one Stryker.

LIGHT METAL

Just because the C-5 and the C-17 are bigger than the Hercules does not make them better. The Hercules can reach its destination faster than the other planes. In addition, there are many places where large planes cannot land. They need long landing strips and hard runways. The Hercules can land on a small runway. It can even land on a runway made of dirt.

For this reason, the Hercules is the most commonly used airplane in the world. It can carry up to 38,000 pounds (17,237 kilograms). A single Stryker weighs 36,240 pounds (16,438 kg), about 18 tons (16 metric tons). Compare this to a tank, which weighs about 60 tons (54 metric tons). A tank is too heavy to be carried by the Hercules. The Stryker's weight makes the Hercules a usable transport vehicle. The Stryker can be flown into battle on the Hercules and rolled out the back of it, fully ready for combat. This cannot be accomplished with a tank or other heavy vehicle.

MIGHT IN SHINING ARMOR

Another important feature of the Stryker is its armor. The Stryker's armor can stop powerful 50-caliber bullets that are bigger than most machine gun or rifle bullets. The armor also protects soldiers from exploding cannon shells.

On top of the Stryker's steel armor lies another layer called appliqué armor. This lightweight ceramic armor gets its name from the French verb "to apply." It can be easily added and removed from a vehicle and is able to withstand armor-piercing bullets. The Stryker does not carry this type of armor all the time because it increases its weight enough to make it impossible for transport by the Hercules.

SLAT ARMOR

Rocket-propelled grenades continue to pose major danger to any vehicle. They are easy to find and buy, and they are cheap, which makes them a commonly used weapon all over the world. To protect the Stryker against this threat, the U.S. Army installed a new type of armor called slat armor.

Slat armor looks like a birdcage. It wraps all the way around the vehicle. It sticks out about 18 inches (46 centimeters) from the Stryker's main armor and is made of wire mesh. If a rocket-propelled grenade hits the slat armor, it explodes without ever touching the vehicle. This protects both the Stryker and the soldiers inside from harm.

Several Strykers, surrounded by protective slat armor, patrol a dangerous area of Iraq.

The army plans to add reactive armor to the Stryker, too. Reactive armor triggers an explosion of its own when a missile hits it. The explosion actually repels, or pushes, the missile away from the vehicle. The soldiers inside are protected because the missile cannot penetrate the hard shell of the Stryker.

FEWER REPAIRS

All vehicles need to be fixed sometimes, but there are no stores to buy replacement parts in a war zone. The Stryker was designed with this consideration in mind. The Stryker's engine is called the Caterpillar. The army uses the Caterpillar engine in many of its combat vehicles, so spare engines and parts are readily available. As a result, fewer mechanics have to go into the war zone to do repairs. It also means that mechanics don't need as much special training to work on the Strykers because they are so similar to other familiar vehicles.

THINK TANK

The Stryker has a state-of-the-art communications system. It's called the Force XXI Battle Command

Brigade and Below (FBCB2). The system lets one Stryker talk to another Stryker using text messages. These are easier to understand than radio messages, which can break up in transmission. The FBCB2 system also lets all Strykers view the same digital map that the commander uses. It shows the position of every vehicle on the battlefield. The commander can mark the enemy forces directly on the map. Each Stryker in the unit can see the same marks on their computer screen, making it easier to understand what is happening.

LONG-DISTANCE VISION

The Stryker's driver uses a periscope similar to a submarine's to see the road ahead of him. The periscope lets him see the road without giving the enemy a chance to shoot. The Stryker features a modern piece of equipment called the driver's vision enhancer (DVE). The DVE is a heat-sensing computer system that lets the driver see faraway objects outside the vehicle. He can view a person standing 394 feet (120 meters) away and a parked vehicle from 3,937 feet (1200 m) away.

A mortar round is fired out of a tube aboard the Mortar Carrier version of the Stryker

chapter 4

STRYKER FORCE

There are two main types of Stryker: the Infantry Carrier Vehicle (ICV) and the Mobile Gun System (MGS). The ICV can transport a nine-man infantry squad as well as their equipment. It has a crew of two, a driver and a vehicle commander. The ICV is able to provide firepower to an infantry squad even when they are not inside the vehicle. The MGS provides the power of a tank, but not the size and weight. Its main gun is a 105 mm tank cannon.

The MGS also has a 50-caliber machine gun, two M6 smoke grenade launchers, and can fire a missile every six seconds. Its gunner uses three periscopes. This equipment lets him see as well on a dark night as he could on a bright day. The MGS is a powerful addition to the BCT team.

In addition to these two basic models, the Stryker currently has eight other versions being used on the battlefield. Each one has a different mission and a different use. Some of the most important new Strykers include:

• **The Medical Evacuation Vehicle (MEV)**, a battlefield ambulance that carries wounded soldiers to a place where doctors can help them.

• **The Mortar Carrier (MC)** version, which uses heavy mortars. A mortar is a very short cannon that fires rockets or shells into the air. These mortars are almost as good as field artillery, large powerful guns that have been mounted on wheels. The mortars are fired through doors that open on the Stryker's roof.

• **The Engineer Support Vehicle (ESV)** that can build roads or clear obstacles.

• **The Antitank Guided Missile (ATGM)**. This type of Stryker can destroy enemy tanks and other heavy vehicles by using guided missiles.

• **The Stryker Reconnaissance Vehicle (RV)**, which looks for the enemy and reports its location to other Strykers. Once it finds its target, it launches missiles to destroy it.

• **A version that locates chemical threats.** Chemical weapons are very dangerous.

This Stryker carries special equipment with chemical sensors. Alarms will activate if they detect chemical weapons. This Stryker has an airtight design so its crew remains safe inside.

Though other types of Strykers will eventually join the BCT, they are not meant to replace tanks and other heavy armored vehicles. They are designed to travel into areas, such as cities, where tanks cannot.

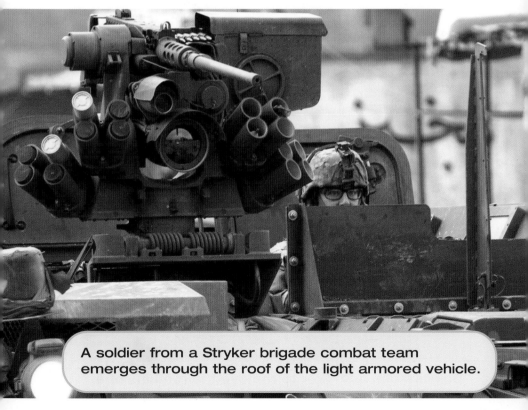

A soldier from a Stryker brigade combat team emerges through the roof of the light armored vehicle.

Soldiers use a Stryker to remove the remains of a vehicle destroyed by a car bomb the previous day.

chapter 5

UNDER FIRE

There are many opinions regarding the Stryker and its combat effectiveness. The Stryker's supporters believe it to be the first step toward a lighter army unit. Critics say it is a waste of money that could endanger soldiers' lives. The Stryker arrived in Iraq in 2003, but was recalled from duty early on to be fitted with slat armor to protect it from rocket-propelled grenade attacks. The Stryker, however, is too wide to enter the C-130 Hercules when the slat armor is attached.

As a result, the armor has to be reattached after the Stryker reaches its destination. This could take as long as 20 minutes. In a war zone, this might not be enough time when faced with the possibility of a sudden attack. Critics also claim that wheeled vehicles such as the Stryker have many disadvantages when compared to tracked vehicles such as tanks. Rubber wheels are more easily damaged than metal tracks.

After being arrested by U.S. troops, several terrorists aboard the Stryker are transported to a nearby detention facility.

Defenders of the Stryker program feel that its merits outweigh its disadvantages. In 2004, terrorists in Iraq fired four rocket-propelled grenades at a Stryker. Three of the missiles missed. The fourth hit the Stryker above the slat armor cage. Even though the rocket-propelled grenade hit above the cage, the Stryker suffered only minor damage. The soldiers inside the Stryker had headaches and one had a small cut. Otherwise, they were not hurt at all. They were able to use the Stryker to chase their attackers.

SNEAK ATTACK

Terrorists in Iraq often use improvised explosive devices (IEDs). IEDs come in all shapes and sizes. They usually take the form of a detonator attached to a bomb or some other explosive. The enemy plants the bomb next to a road and explodes it when a vehicle passes close by. The most common type of IED is military ammunition like an artillery or mortar shell. These are cheap, easy to make, and they can cause a lot of damage—even death—when used properly.

One of the biggest dangers to soldiers in Iraq just now is the improvised explosive device, or IED (see sidebar above). So far, the Stryker appears to be up to this challenge. In 2004, a Stryker brigade came under attack. Explosions from IEDs hit two Strykers. One blast blew a

wheel off one Stryker. Another explosion caused an engine fire that forced soldiers to exit the vehicle. Despite the damage, there were no serious injuries to either crew.

THE ROAD AHEAD

The military continues to prepare for the future. One of the army's goals is to send help anywhere in the world in a very short period. Brigade combat teams will enable the army to do this—

Although the Stryker has received much criticism from its opponents, there are many who praise its effectiveness in combat.

BCTs can be moved quickly. Heavy tanks can take thirty days to get to a location. Heavier units might take even longer. Until the tanks arrive, BCTs must fight and win on their own. The Stryker makes such missions more than possible.

The Stryker swiftly patrols hostile areas while protecting itself and the soldiers inside. Quite simply, it lets the army fight and win.

STRYKER ICV

At a Glance

50-caliber heavy machine gun

Gun turret

Hatch

Ceramic-skin armor

GENERAL CHARACTERISTICS

PRIMARY FUNCTION: TROOP TRANSPORT/ATTACK	WEAPONS: REMOTE-CONTROLLED GUN TURRET, 50-CALIBER HEAVY MACHINE GUN, 7.62 MM MACHINE GUN, 40 MM JAVELIN MISSILE LAUNCHERS
CONTRACTOR: GENERAL DYNAMICS LAND SYSTEMS	
POWER: 1 CATERPILLAR TURBODIESEL ENGINE	HEIGHT: 9 FEET (3 METERS)
COST: $1.3–2 MILLION	WEIGHT: 36,240 POUNDS (16,438 KG)
CREW: TWO	SPEED: 60 MILES (97 KM) PER HOUR

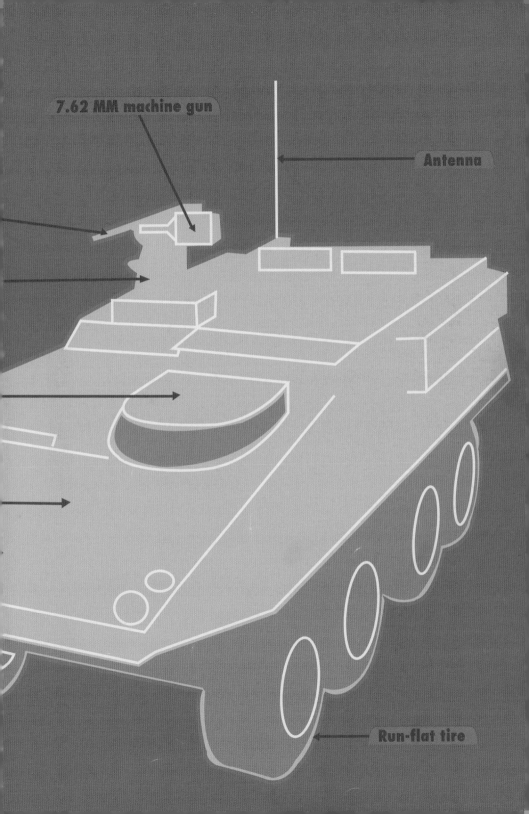

7.62 MM machine gun

Antenna

Run-flat tire

NEW WORDS

appliqué armor (ap-li-**kay ar**-mur) ceramic armor added to steel armor of a military vehicle

artillery (ar-**til**-uh-ree) large, powerful guns mounted on wheels or tracks

brigade (bri-**gayd**) a unit of an army

caliber (**kal**-uh-buhr) size of a bullet or shell

communism (**kom**-yuh-niz-uhm) a way of organizing a country so that all the lands, houses, factories, etc. belong to the government or community, and the profits are shared by all

deflate (di-**flate**) to let the air out of something

digital (**dij**-uh-tuhl) expressed in digits, especially with computers

fascism (**fash**-iz-uhm) a form of government in which a dictator and his party have complete power over a country

firepower (**fire**-pow-uhr) the capacity to deliver fire

NEW WORDS

guerilla (guh-**ril**-uh) a member of a small group of fighters who launch surprise attacks against an official army

infantry (**in**-fuhn-tree) the part of an army that fights on foot

inflate (in-**flate**) to make something expand by blowing air into it

mortar (**mor**-tuhr) a short cannon that fires shells or rockets high in the air

paratrooper (**pa**-ruh-troo-puhr) a soldier trained to jump by parachute

periscope (**per**-uh-skope) a tube with mirrors at each end that allows you to see something from a position below

reconnaissance (ri-**kon**-e-sans) gathering information by observation

runway (**ruhn**-way) a strip of level land that aircraft use for taking off and landing

terrain (tuh-**rayn**) ground or land

FOR FURTHER READING

Anderson, Christopher J. *Hell on Wheels: The Men of the U.S. Armored Forces, 1918 to the Present.* Mechanicsburg, PA: Stackpole Books, 1999.

Anderson, Christopher J. *The U. S. Army Today: From the End of the Cold War to the Present Day.* London: Greenhill Books, 1997.

Doherty, Kieran. *Congressional Medal of Honor Recipients.* Berkeley Heights, NJ: Enslow Publishers Inc., 1998.

Yancey, Diane. *Iraq War: The Homefront.* Farmington Hills, MI: Lucent Books, 2004.

ORGANIZATIONS

The Congressional Medal of Honor
Museum and Society
40 Patriots Point Road
Mt. Pleasant, SC 29464-4377
(843) 884-8862
http://www.cmohs.org/society/museum.htm

The United States Air Force
Chief of Public Relations
1040 Air Force Pentagon
Washington, DC 20330-1040
www.af.mil

The United States Army
Chief of Public Affairs
1500 Army Pentagon
Washington, DC 20310-1500
www.army.mil

RESOURCES

WEB SITES

ARMY TECHNOLOGY

www.army-technology.com
This site provides updates with photos of new military technologies and where they are being used.

MEDAL OF HONOR

www.medalofhonor.com
This official Web site contains the history, names, and citations of every member of the military who ever received the Congressional Medal of Honor.

U.S. DEPARTMENT OF DEFENSE

www.defenselink.mil
This Web site contains many photos and articles on a wide range of military equipment.

INDEX

INDEX

ABOUT THE AUTHORS

Larry Hama is a veteran of the U.S. Army who lives in New York City. He currently works as a freelance writer and cartoonist and is best known for his work for Marvel Comics.

Bill Cain is a U.S. Army colonel in military intelligence who lives in Atlanta, Georgia. He is a two-time combat veteran of the Iraq Wars and has over twenty-five years of army experience.